Prayers of the Highlanders

Prayers of the Western Highlanders

A New Collection

G. R. D. McLean

First published in Great Britain in 2008

Society for Promoting Christian Knowledge
36 Causton Street
London SW1P 4ST

British Library Cataloguing-in-Publication Data
A catalogue record for this book is available from the British Library

ISBN 978–0–281–05985–0

1 3 5 7 9 10 8 6 4 2

Typeset by Graphicraft Ltd, Hong Kong
Printed in Great Britain by Ashford Colour Press

Produced on paper from sustainable forests

Contents

Foreword

In 1961, while searching for methods of prayer that would be useful to teenagers and new Christians, I came across G. R. D. McLean's *Poems of the Western Highlanders*. This was a revelation to me: a whole corpus of literature from the Hebrides that had been handed down by word of mouth. I was immediately attracted by the rhythm and the earthiness of the prayers, which offered a less formalized and more natural way of conversing with God.

G. R. D. McLean's source was *Carmina Gadelica*, hymns and prayers of the Western Highlanders, collected and compiled in the nineteenth century by Alexander Carmichael. For a good while, I have known that G. R. D. McLean left manuscript copies of further translations, and it was with great pleasure that I heard that a collection of these was to be published under the title *Prayers of the Western Highlanders*.

To open *Prayers of the Western Highlanders* is to enter a world of faith and meet a people who have dedicated mind, will, soul and body to God. 'The Trinity Consecration' shows an ease and a delight in the Holy Three. 'New-born' is a reminder that mortality in childbirth was high, and the women who helped in birth often said such a prayer to immerse the new-born in divine care. 'Safe-keeping' reflects upon the protection and liberating power of the Trinity.

Prayers of the Western Highlanders deserves to be read and enjoyed by as many people as possible. Its wealth of prayer – rooted in the petitions of those who are at home with God and welcome him into every area of their lives – will be of much value to those of us seeking to develop a prayer life of our own. Here we encounter the encircling love of God as we dwell in him and he in us. This is treasure indeed.

David Adam

Note on the Text

In *Prayers of the Western Highlanders*, G. R. D. McLean offers translations of typical Gaelic poems, chosen from folklorist Alexander Carmichael's massive collection, *Carmina Gadelica*.

GOD THE FATHER

O Father Creator and great High Chief,
Commander of human love and belief,
What time the world and the oceans began
Thou didst ordain the first making of man
   In a garden place
   Enfolded by grace.

O Father Creator and Chief of might,
Who didst send thy Son for the latter plight,
The angels came down proclaiming thy voice,
From the cloud was heard thy determined choice
   As came forth of old
   The commandments told.

O Father Creator and Chief all wise,
Unto thee was offered the sacrifice,
And thou didst behold from thy Judgement throne
The lifted tree of the cross to atone,
   The victory won
   By thine only Son.

O Father Creator and Chief of life,
Thine is the Spirit for stilling the strife,
Thine is the greatness, the wonder, the power,
Thine is the mountain, the sea, and the flower,
   And thine is the love
   That comes from above.

O Father Creator and Chief of praise,
Thine are the songs that the holy ones raise,

Thine are the souls that the angels befriend,
Thine is the city where life has no end,
> *Where grace has no cease,*
> *The far strand of peace.*

COMMENDATION PRAYER

O our God and Chief, in the morning we make our prayer, God and Chief, this night we make our prayer, for we give unto thee our mind, our will, our wish, our soul everlasting and our body;

Be thou chieftain over us, master unto us, shepherd over us, guardian unto us, herdsman over us, guide unto us, and be thou with us, O Chief of Chiefs, Father everlasting, and God of the heavens, who reignest for ever and ever. Amen.

CREDO

I believe in the God of all gods, the eternal Father of life and of love, the eternal Father of the holy and of each person, the eternal Father of the children of men and of the world; and I believe in the Chief and God of the spirits of men, who created the heaven above, the dome of the skies, and the ocean beneath, who created and warped the soul, giving it a possession, and from dust and ashes created the body, giving it breath.*

O Father, bless to me my body and my soul, my life and my belief.

I believe in the eternal Father and Chief of the spirits of men, who bound my soul in the Spirit of healing, who gave his loved Son in covenant for me, who purchased my soul for his Son's precious blood; and I believe in the eternal Father and Chief of life who poured his spirit of grace upon me at my baptizing.

O eternal Father and Chief of men, enwrapping my body and my dear soul, keep me safe this night in thy love's sanctuary and shelter me with the aiding of the saints; for thou hast brought me up from the night that is past to the gracious light of this day, to provide great joy for my soul and do good most excellent for me: Thanks be unto thee, Christ Jesu, for the many gifts bestowed, each day, each night, each sea and land, each weather fair, each mild, each rough.

I give to thee the whole worship of my life, the whole assent of my power, the whole praise of my tongue, the whole honour of my speaking; I give to thee the whole reverence of my understanding, the whole offering of my thought, the whole laud of my fervour, the humility of the blood of the Lamb; and I give to thee the whole love of my devotion, the whole kneeling of my desire, the whole affection of my heart, the whole kindness of my sense, the whole breathing of my mind, and all my soul, O God of all gods.

I beseech thee keep my thought and deed, my word and will, my understanding and wisdom, my way and state, keep them from ill and hurt and harm, from misfortune and from grief, and keep me this night in the nearness of thy love; and finally may God shield me and fill, hold me and watch, and bring me to the place of peace, the land of the King, the peace of eternity.

All praise be to the Father and to the Son and to the Holy Ghost, the Three in One, God for evermore. Amen.

*Warped. In weaving, to warp is to arrange the threads which are extended length-wise in the loom.

THE ARM OF GOD

O everlasting Father, do thou thyself take us in thine own generous clasp. Laying us in thine own generous arm, for the sake of Jesus Christ thy Son our Lord. Amen.

PETITION AGAINST NIGHT-FEAR

O God, be thou before us, behind us, above us and below us, we on thy path, thou upon our way; for who, O God and Lord, but thou is there on land, there on wave, there on ocean swell, there by the door, along with us?

We are here abroad, in need, in pain, in distress, and all alone; grant us therefore thine aid, O God, through Jesus Christ thy Son our Lord. Amen.

GIFTS OF THE FATHER

O Father of heaven, the wisdom of serpent, of raven, and of mighty
eagle be ours:
The voice of swan, of honey, and of the Son of the stars:
The plenty of the sea, of the land, and thine own plenty,
Through Jesus Christ our Lord. Amen.

THE ENTRUSTING OF THE FATHER

O dear Father of mercifulness, who dost set us in the care of an angel of God to make round us the shepherding of the fold of the saints this night:

Grant that he may drive off from us each temptation and danger, surround us on the ocean of unrighteousness, and in the narrows, crooks and straits hold our own coracle in his keeping;

May he be a bright flame before us, a guiding star over us, a smooth path under us, and a loving shepherd behind us, today, tonight and for ever,

That when we are weary and strangers we be led to the land of the angels; since time it is for us to go home unto the court of Christ, unto the peace of heaven, through the name of Jesus Christ our Lord. Amen.

GOD THE SON

Shepherd of the field,
Jesus, thou our shield,
By thy wounding healed,
Master, Lord of angel host,
Feed us, lead us coast to coast,
Jesus, weald to weald
By the lamb-blood sealed.

Prayer to thee we raise
As the cattle graze,
Round thy beauty stays,
Herdsman great without a son,
Circler of our folding-in;
We would give thee praise
All our length of days.

Branch of glory strong
Shading us from wrong,
To our heart belong;
Kindness by the woodland there,
Son of Mary gentle fair,
With the angel-throng
Make we now our song.

Rook of truth so tall, *
Living waterfall,
Mercy's spring for all
Son of God of healing hand
Nigh us in temptation's land,
Hear us when we call,
Be to us a wall.

Kindler of the light
Of the star-spread night,
Door of joys' delight,
Guide and open thou our way,
Lantern shining to the day,
Christ above the height,
Fade not from our sight.

*Rook (cf. ruck, rick). A heap or pile.

TO CHRIST OF THE STARS

O thou Lightener of the stars, on the crests of the clouds we behold thee, the choristers of the sky singing thy name as thou dost descend with a merry noise from the Father above, harp and lyre of song making music to thee;

O Christ, refuge of our love, why should we not lift thy fame while angels and holy ones of melody sing thy name?

Thou Son of Mary of the virtues, of exceeding fair-white beauty, joy it were to us to be in the meadow of thy richness;

O Christ our beloved, O Christ of the Holy Blood, by day and by night we sing thy name, for thine own sake. Amen.

A CHRISTMAS DOXOLOGY

All glory be to the King, for that on this night of great birth he was born the Son of the Virgin Mary, his feet brought down to the earth, the Son of virtues from on high, heaven and earth giving him light:

The peace of earth is his, his joy of heaven, as lo, his feet touch the ground:

A royal feu,* a lamb's welcome are his, King of the virtues, Lamb of the glories, land and sea shining to him, shining to him moor and field, the sound of the waves on the beach of the shore telling that Christ is born;

Christ is born Son of the King of kings from the land of salvation, and the sun shines to him on the mountain-tops, the earth and the world together shine to him as God the Lord opens the door:

O Son of the Virgin Mary, hasten thou to help us, thou Christ of hope, thou Door of joy, golden Sun of range and hill:

Unto thee, the King of our song, be all glory and blessing and joy. Amen.

*Feu. Tribute.

CHRIST'S BLESSING

Be the beauty of Christ towards us, the beauty of Christ to us; be the beauty of Christ before us, the beauty of Christ behind us; be the beauty of Christ over us, the beauty of Christ under us; be the beauty of Christ with us, the beauty of Christ around us, of a Monday and a Sunday; be the beauty of Christ around us of a Monday and a Sunday. Amen.

SELF-DEDICATION PRAYER

O Jesu, thou Son of Mary, have mercy upon us; O Jesu, thou Son
of Mary, grant us thy peace; be with us and for us when we
come to our long dwelling place; be with us also at the morn-
ing of our setting sail, and at the closing of our life's day, the
dawn and darkness of our brief season; be with us and for us,
O merciful God of all:

Finally we pray thee, O King of kings and God of all, consecrate
our condition and lot, consecrate our rights and means, con-
secrate our heart and body, each heart and body each day to
thee and each night also, who with the Father and Holy Ghost
livest and reignest, world without end. Amen.

PRAYER OF THE SOUL

O Lord Jesus Christ, Herdsman of the poor, Person without sin, who sorely didst suffer by the sentence of wicked men and wast crucified:

Tonight do thou save us from evil, save us from harm, protecting our bodies and sanctifying us tonight, O Jesu, tonight, and leave us not;

Endow us with thy strength, O Herdsman of the virtues, guide us aright, guide us in thy strength, and keep us in thy strength, O Lord Jesus Christ. Amen.

PRAYER FOR LIFE

O Lord Jesus, we pray thee for a life of joy with honour, estate and good name, no sighing from our breast, no tear from our eye; and may there be no hindrance on our path, no shadow upon our face, till we lie down in that walled place beyond in thine arms, O Lord Christ of kindness, where thou rulest always. Amen.

THE ENCOMPASSING OF JESUS

O Jesu, the Lamb, the only begotten Son of God the Father, thou didst give the wine-blood of thy body to purchase us from death, O our Christ, our Christ, who shielded us each day and night, each light and shadowtime:

Be near and uphold us, thou our triumph and our treasure when we lie or stand, when we watch or sleep, O Jesu, Son of Mary, our helper and encircler, O Jesu, Son of David, our strength everlasting, who with the Father and the Holy Ghost livest and reignest, world without end. Amen.

GUIDANCE-BLESSING

O Lord Jesus Christ, Son of the Blessed Virgin Mary, be thyself unto us a steady lantern of kindliness to guide us over the great rough ocean of eternity; we ask this for thy name's sake. Amen.

GOD THE HOLY GHOST

Gently distil, O Holy Ghost, thy grace,
Who first didst move upon the waters' face,
With might to fall upon our human race,
Thy coming as the white descending dove,
His wings spread with faith and hope and love,
Proceeding Holy Spirit from above.

O Holy Ghost, unseen as is the dew,
Our early morning green with strength renew
In generous fullness, Holy Spirit true;
In heat thou art a springing water cold,
Thy wind to aid, thy breath the soul to hold,
Thy gift of life to us is sevenfold.

THE WELL OF THE HOLY GHOST

May the Holy Spirit of God fill us to the brim with all his saving fullness of grace, through Jesus Christ our Lord. Amen.

FOR THE HOLY SPIRIT

O Great Spirit of holiness, come down from the heavenly places as the dew to our aid and to our satisfying, that our prayers fast bound may find acceptance at the throne of the great King of all;

Fill us with thy grace befitting according to the will of the God of all life; and grant that in God's love and affection, his will and his all-seeing eye, his loving purposes and his care, as the angels and the saints and all the company of heaven desire to serve, so may we on earth desire, through Jesus Christ our Lord and Saviour. Amen.

VENI CREATOR SPIRITUS

O Holy Spirit of great might, come down upon us and lay us beneath thy directing and from thy glorious habitation in the heavens pour upon us the brilliance of thy light;

Thou Father beloved of each naked one, from whom all gifts and goodness proceed, brighten our heart with thy mercy, with thy mercy shield us from each evil, for without thy Godhead there is nothing in man worthy of price, and without thyself, O king of kings, man can never be without sin;

In aid thou art best of all against the soul of fiercest words, as food thou art sweetest far of all, sustain us therefore and guide us always:

Thou who dost heal, loosen the neck (knee) that is stiff, warm beneath thy wing the heart that is hard, and grasp the helm of the soul that wanders from thy path, that he die not;

Each thing that is foul be swift to cleanse, each thing that is hard be gracious to soften, each wound that causes us pain, O Healer of healers, do thou make whole;

And grant that we thy people be diligent to put our trust in thee as God, that thou help us with thy sevenfold gift each hour, O generous Holy Spirit, who with the Father and the Son abidest one God, world without end. Amen.

PRAYER FOR SAFETY

O thou healer of our soul, keep us evening, morning and noon-
tide as we fare our rough course, helping and guarding our
possessions this night; for we are tired and astray and our foot-
steps stumble;

Shield us therefore from snare and from sin, for thy name's sake,
Jesus Christ our Lord. Amen.

GOD THE HOLY TRINITY

Seasons come and seasons go,
Tidestreams ebb and tidestreams flow,
Father, Son, and Holy Ghost
Fill the days and cleanse the coast.

Storms and winds and waves arise,
Mists and sunrays clothe the skies,
Father, Son, and Holy Ghost,
Three in One have power the most.

Spring renews the yearly life,
Man has work and peace and strife,
Father, Son, and Holy Ghost
Reign the Three unchanging host.

BLESSING FOR EACH DAY

The blessing of God be upon you, that good come to you; the blessing of Christ be upon you, that good be done to you; the blessing of the Holy Ghost be yours, that good be the course of your life, each day of your arising, each night of your lying down, for evermore. Amen.

THE THREE

O Holy Trinity, who art both overhead and underfoot, who art above both here and beyond, who pervadest the earth, the air, and the heavens, and who dwellest also in the great breakers of the vast sea, be the knowledge of thy presence with us this day and always. Amen.

PREPARATION PRAYER

O Father Creator, Son Redeemer, and Spirit Cleanser, of friendship and love, we bend in prayer before thy sight:

Grant to us fully in our need a love towards God, and the affection, the smile, the wisdom, the grace, and the fear that are his, that we may do his will in the world of the Trinity, as do the angels and saints in heaven;

Finally do thou each day of cloud or of brightness, each day, each night, each time, in thy kindness give us thy nature, O God, through thine own Anointed One, Jesus Christ our Lord. Amen.

TRIPLE ENCOMPASSING

O God, be thy sanctuary around us, thy sanctuary, O God of life;

O Christ, be thy sanctuary around us, thy sanctuary, O Christ of love;

O Spirit, be thy sanctuary around us, thy sanctuary, O Spirit Holy;

O Trinity, be thy sanctuary around us, thy sanctuary, O gracious Trinity,

To preserve us, preserve us for evermore. Amen.

MORNING PROTECTION

O God, set thine eye between us and each eye, thy purpose between us and each purpose, thy hand between us and each hand, thy shield between us and each shield, thy desire between us and each desire, and thy bridle between us and each bridle, that no mouth may be able to say its curse upon us:

O Christ, set thy pain between us and each pain, thy love between us and each love, thy dearness between us and each dearness, thy kindness between us and each kindness, thy wish between us and each wish, and thy will between us and each will, that no venom may be able to cause us wound: And be thy might between us and each might, O Christ, thy right between us and each right:

O Holy Spirit, set thy flow between us and each flow, thy cleansing between us and each cleansing, thy water between us and each water, that no pollution or evil may be able to touch us,

O Holy Trinity, God everlasting. Amen.

BLESSING OF THE TRINITY

O Holy Trinity, be the eye of God dwelling with us, be the foot of Christ guiding us, be the shower of the Spirit pouring upon us, in all richness and generousness of heart, for the days of our life. Amen.

PILGRIMS' AIDING

May God be with us in the mountain pass, Jesus with us as we
climb, the Spirit with us by the flowing stream, by headland,
ridge and green;

May they be with us by sea and land, by moor and meadow, each
lying-down and arising, in the trough of the waves and on the
crest of the swell, each step of the journey we take; we ask this
for the sake of Jesus Christ our Lord. Amen.

THE TRINITY OF STRENGTH

O great Trinity of strength, we place our souls and our bodies under
   thy protection this night;

And may the Father and the Son and the gentle Spirit be our shield
   and shelter, who live and reign for ever. Amen.

THY NEIGHBOUR AS THYSELF

Kindness in our face
And the Spirit's grace;
Wisdom in our speech
As we speak to each;
O Lord Christ, thou art
Love within the heart;
In love may we greet
Though a foe we meet.

NEW YEAR BLESSING

O God, bless to us the new day never devised ere this for us, for it is to bless thine own presence with us that thou hast given us this time, O God;

And bless to us our looking; may we bless all we see; our neighbours may we bless, our neighbours blessing us;

And finally, O God, give unto us a clean heart, nor let us from the sight of thine eye, blessing to us children and partners, blessing to us livelihood and cattle-stock, through Jesus Christ our Lord. Amen.

INVOCATION FOR GRACE

O God, set thy beauty in our face, thy Son to protect us from the
evil ones of the world, the King of the stars before us:

Since it is the Blessed Mary and Jesus her Son who gave the fair
look to our countenance, be the taste of gentle honey upon us
and upon each word that we utter, to low and high, to man and
woman gentle, from this day now until the end of our life;

We ask this in the bosom-kindness of love and the powers ever-
lasting, in the kindness of the God of life, and in the kindness
of his Son who doth clothe us, for ever. Amen.

REQUEST OF THE PILGRIMS' HOPE

O Son of God, be mercy upon our tongue, be kindness upon our countenance, be chasteness upon our desire, be wisdom upon our wishing:

The love that Mary gave to thee, her one Son, let all the world give unto us, the love that thou didst give to the Baptist John, grant we give to those who meet us:

And be thou at the beginning of our journey, be thou the trust of our aiding, do thou clear our path, do thou be at the end of our travelling, O Son of God, to whom be glory for ever. Amen.

PEACE BLESSING

O Christ, O King of all, in thy love let there be peace between neigh-
bours, peace between kindred, peace between lovers; peace also
between man and man, husband and wife, mother and children,
thy peace, O Christ, above all peace:

O Christ, bless our face that it give blessing, and our eye that it
give blessing to all that it beholds; we ask this for thy name's
sake. Amen.

THE PRESENCE

Grant, O Father, I see
Those who lie down with me,
God of all life they be,
King, Son, Spirit, the Three.

Grant, O Jesus, I know
Thy wonder-birth below,
The grace thy words bestow,
Thy blood's forgiving flow.

Grant, O Spirit, I feel
Thy life-power to be real,
Thy breath to give the seal,
Thy hand to save and heal.

Grant, O Three, I awake
My prayer to thee to make
My daily path to take,
To live for thy dear sake.

God grant me Bread and Wine,
The Christ-life that is thine,
Partaking of it mine,
The sustenance divine.

THE EYES OF VISION

Be God before us, God behind us, be God over us, be we on God's path, be God in our footsteps:

O Son of the King of life, be thou our support after us, to give us the eyes of our vision, thy love in front of us, thy grace undimmed, thy death before our eyes always. Amen.

BLOOD-BROTHERHOOD WITH US

O Jesus, King of graces, in the time of stress and of strain, when but feeble is our strength and vigour, do thou make brotherhood with us in thy precious blood, for thy name's sake. Amen.

THE GIFT OF THE SON

Thanks be to God for the gift of the Son of the dawn and of the clouds, of the sphere and of the star;

For the Son of the rain and of the dew, of the firmament and of the sky;

For the Son of the fire and of the light, of the earth and of the world;

For the Son of the elements and of the heavens, of the moon and of the sun;

For the Son of Mary of God's favour, for the Son of God the good news of speech;

Thanks be to God for the gift. Amen.

THE INCARNATION GLORY

Glory be to God at this hour,

For lo, the Virgin comes, the Christ so young at her breast, the angels bowing low before them, the King of life declaring it must be:

The Virgin, dew-gold her tresses, the Jesus than snow more white, the seraphim of melody praising them with song, the King of life declaring it must be:

Glory be to God. Amen.

BORN IN THE STABLE

O Child of joy, Child of Mary, born in the stable King of life, who
    didst go into the wilderness and in our place didst suffer, be
    they reckoned happy who are near to thee;

For when they didst see that we were beset, the heavens opened
    with grace over our head, and we did see Christ, the Spirit of
    truth, who drew us beneath the shield of his crown;

Strengthen our hope, give life to our joy, keep us mighty, true and
    close, thou Light of our lantern, as with the virgins we sing in
    glory the new song. Amen.

PRAYER FOR GOD'S AID

God be my unfolding and God my enclosing; God in my speaking and God my thinking; God in my sleep and God awake; God in my looking and God my hope; God in my life and God my lips; God in my soul and God my heart; God my sufficing and God be my rest; God my immortality, God mine everlasting. Amen.

NIGHT BLESSING OF GOD'S PRESENCE

O blessed Trinity, we lie down tonight as is fitting in the companionship of Christ the Son of the Virgin of the looks, in the companionship of the gracious Father of glory, in the companionship of the aiding Spirit of power:

We lie down tonight with God, God tonight lying down as we do, we lie not down tonight with evil, no evil or mark of it lying down with us:

We lie down tonight with the Holy Spirit, the Holy Spirit lying down as we do, we lie down tonight with the Three of our affection, the Three of our affection lying down as we do, to whom be glory for ever and ever. Amen.

THE TRINITY CONSECRATION

Grant, O God, that this night we rest with thee, that thou rest with
    us;
That this night we rest with Christ, that Christ rest with us;
That this night we rest with the Spirit, that the Spirit rest with us;
That thou and Christ and the Spirit rest with us,
For the same Jesus Christ's sake. Amen.

THE SANCTUARY OF PROTECTION

Who before us but our God and our Lord, who behind us, and who beneath us? Who is our stay but the Three of might, Father, Son and gentle Spirit?

O God and O Lord Jesus, O Holy Trinity, bless us evermore. Amen.

NEW-BORN

A moon is new in beauty of grace,
A life is new in sweetness of face,
A tide flows new with its cleansing trace,
A holy water glistens in place.

The Spirit descends, a holy dove,
Shedding a grace and a holy love,
With a cleansing drop from God above
From spirits of evil shield enough.

The Father's mark on the brow is worn,
The Saviour's mark of his cross of scorn,
The Spirit's mark of the living dawn,
In name of the Three-in-One new-born.

TRINITY BLESSING

The blessing of God and of the Lord be upon you, the blessing also of the perfect Spirit upon you; the blessing of the Holy Trinity to pour upon you in mild and generous flow, in mild and generous flow, O Three in One, God for evermore. Amen.

DOXOLOGY OF THE WATERS

As it was and is and shall be evermore, O Threefold God of grace, as ebbs and as flows the tide, O Threefold God of grace, as the tide ebbs and flows evermore. Amen.

GRACE FROM GOD

Grace us, O God, as thou the world doth grace,
Grace us with goodness of the land and sea,
And grace us with thy presence in each place
That we thy heartfelt worshippers may be.

Grace us, O God, as thou dost sinners grace,
Grace of forgiveness, grace of cleansing stream,
Grace us with justice and with mercy's face,
That graced we stand before the balanced beam.

Grace us, O God, as thou dost grace a night
With thy fair lamp of grace, a darkness guide,
Grace us with seven satisfyings' might
That healed, made perfect, we with thee abide.

PRAYER FOR GRACE

O Saviour of grace, in the eye of the Father Creator, the Son Redeemer, and the Spirit Purifier, we bend before thee in prayer of love:

From thy high place of the heavenly City pour down upon us thy riches, thy blessing, thy forgiveness in all patience;

And grant us, O Saviour of glory, the fear and the love divine, the lovingness and the will divine ever to perform on earth after the heavenly manner of angels and saints, with thy peace each day and night, thy peace each day and night, for ever and ever. Amen.

THE DEW OF GRACE

May the grace of God and of Christ and of the Holy Spirit be shed upon us as the dew, each day and each night of our span in this world, each day and each night of our span in this world, henceforth and for evermore. Amen.

DAILY ASPIRATION

O God, grant each day thy justice, each day thy righteous wisdom
to the tongue, each day the marks of thy correcting, each day
and night the peace that is with thee;

Each day grant, O God, that we reckon thy mercy's causes, give
heed each day unto thy laws, each day a song composing thee,
each day the music of thy glory sounding;

And to thy Son Lord Jesus grant each day we bring love, the night
season also; each day and night, shadow-black or shining, grant
we praise thy goodness to us, O God, for evermore. Amen.

MIGHT AND GOODNESS

O Saviour, be ours the might of the raven, of the eagle, of the knights
of old; be ours the might of storm, of the moon, of the sun;
be ours the might of the sea, of the earth, of the sky:

The goodness of the sea, the goodness of the earth, the good-
ness of the sky be ours; each day be of happiness, no day be of
sorrow, honour and mercy be ours; each face have love for us,
death on our bed be ours, thou our Saviour with us, for ever.
Amen.

THE STEERING OF GOD

O God, do thou steer with thy wisdom, correct with thy justice, assist with thy mercy, and protect with thy strength;

With thy fullness do thou fill us, with thine overshadowing do thou shield us, and with thy grace fill us again, for the sake of thine Anointed Son of royal David's seed, who did visit his Temple, who in the garden was offered Lamb and Sacrifice, who died on our behalf, Jesus Christ our Lord. Amen.

BLESSING OF THE GRACE OF GOD

The grace of God, and of our Lord Jesus Christ, and of the Holy Spirit be with us and with our children for the time that is now, that is to come, and that shall ever be, world without end. Amen.

CHIEF OF CHIEFS

O Chief of chiefs, thy Godhead be with us when we lie down or rise up, in each ray of light, in each single joy of ours;

Thy Christ Son be with us when we sleep or wake or watch each day and night through;

God our protecting, the Lord our directing, the Spirit our strength, for ever and evermore. Amen.

PENITENCE

O Lord, abate
Thy wrath above,
Our sins are great,
Greater thy love.

O Lord forgive,
Mercy decree,
Judged may we live,
Judged but by thee.

O Lord, renew,
Our stumbling cease,
Thy way is true,
True is our peace.

O Lord of tear,
Sorrow thou art,
Sorrow is here
Within our heart.

APPEAL UNTO GOD

O God, we make our appeal to the Father who did shape all flesh, and to Christ who did suffer scorn and pain, and to the Spirit who will heal our wound, to make us white as the cotton-grass of the moorland, through the same Jesus Christ our Lord. Amen.

RISING PRAYER

O King of the moon and of the sun and of the stars in thy lovely fragrance, it is thou who knowest our needs, thou who art the merciful God of all things;

For each day of our movement, each time of our awakening we cause the shadow of displeasure to pass over the countenance of the King of hosts who loved us;

O be with us through each day, with us through each night, be with us each night and day, with us each day and night, O King of kings, God evermore. Amen.

PRAYER FOR FORGIVENESS

O God, be with us this thy day (this thy night), be with us and towards us, Amen; for we have merited thine anger from our first day, thine own anger, O God of all:

O God, forgive; O God, forgive with thine own forgiveness, in thy mercy, Amen;

And grant that those things which are evil in us, those things which may witness against us in the day of our long abiding, be made clear to us, be kept dark from us, be estranged utterly from us, and chased from our hearts, for ever and evermore. Amen.

CONFESSION PRAYER

O Lord Jesu, grant us thy forgiveness of sins and that we be
mindful of our wickedness; grant us thy grace of repentance,
forgiveness and of obedience, of sincerity and humility, that at
this time we make confession freely, that at its seat we condemn
ourselves lest we be condemned at the seat of judgement.

Grant to us the strength and courage for the same; for it is
easier for us to be chastened for a season than for eternity to
go to death; wherefore, O Jesu, grant that we confess our
wickedness thoroughly as at death's threshold:

Jesu, take pity on us, have mercy upon us; take us unto thee and
aid our souls; for sin is a cause of grief, and a cause of anguish
is death, but of joy is repentance a cause and washing in the
stream-waters of salvation; and there will be joy also among the
angels of heaven that we are bathed in the pool of confession:

Rejoice therefore, O my soul, for God wills thy reconciling; seize
hold upon his outstretched hand to tell thee of a reconciling
of love:

Finally refuse not thy hand to us, O God, refuse not thy hand, O
Lord of lords, and let us not go to eternal death, for the sake
of the same Jesus Christ our Saviour. Amen.

DAY BY DAY

Each day, O God, give gladness with thy dawn,
Each day, O God, to wonted tasks we rise,
Each day, O God, we kneel to thee, new-born
The little lovely Christ who grace supplies.

Each day we thank thee for the food we take,
Each day, O God, we offer prayer and praise,
Each step be thine, each dealing that we make,
Each morning hour, each hour of all our days.

Each day, O God, the noontide light is thine,
Each day, O God, our house with warmth is blest,
Each day be nigh, O God of Bread and Wine,
Each day thy shielding o'er us gently rest.

Each day, O God, as shadow-eventide
Descends upon us, calling to repose,
Each day thy peace upon us to abide
Until our day draws to its lasting close.

PEACE-BLESSING UNTO THE END

The peace of God and of Christ and of the Holy Spirit be present with us and with our children from this day forward to the very ending day of our lives, until comes the ending day of our lives. Amen.

MORNING SUPPLICATION

O Being of life, of peace, of time, of eternity, keep fair our portion, our desire, and our lot, better than we know to ask; shepherd us this day and relieve our plight, enfold us this night and pour upon us thy grace;

Finally guard our tongue, strengthen our love, lighten our path to the stream and succour us in our death, through Jesus Christ our Lord. Amen.

PRAYER FOR THE HOUSEHOLD

Bless, O God, the world and all that is therein, the partner of our life, the children of our care; and bless the watching eye of our head, and the things our hands do, from the early morn of rising to the late evening of taking rest:

Protect, O God, our house and those within our threshold, consecrate our children tended, and enfold the flocks and young; do thou follow after them and shepherd them, from the time when the herd goes up to hill and lea to the time of lying down to sleep, through Jesus Christ our Lord. Amen.

THANKSGIVING FOR THE MORNING

O Great God who dost serve and give to all the world, thanks be unto thee for our morning rising to this our life; be it to thy glory, also of our souls;

Grant to our souls, we pray thee, thy merciful aiding, covering them with the shadow of thy wing even as we clothe our bodies;

And help us to avoid all sinning and to forsake all that causes us to sin, from our souls, O God, clearing away each wreath of haze confusing even as the mist scatters upon the hilltops, through Jesus Christ our Lord. Amen.

PRAYER AT DRESSING

Bless, O God, to us our soul and our body, our belief and all our
    state; bless our heart, our speech and the workings of our hand;
    the strength and the duties of the morning; the modest dis-
    position and behaving, the power and the wisdom of thinking;

And bless, O God of virtues, thine own path, until we sleep
    tonight, thine own path until tonight, through Jesus Christ our
    Lord. Amen.

GRACE BEFORE MEALS

O God, be with us when we break bread, be with us when we finish
　our meal;
May our bodies take nothing that may stain our contrite hearts,
　through Jesus Christ our Lord. Amen.

THANKS AFTER MEALS

All thanks and praise and worship be unto thee, O God, for all
that thou hast given unto us, and as thou hast given the life of
our body to win the food of this world, so grant us the life
eternal to show forth thy glory;

Grant us therefore grace throughout life, and life at death's hour;
be with us, O God, when we put off our breath, when we strive
in the deep currents, when breathing and striving we sound the
fords and cross the deep waters, be with us, through Jesus Christ
our Lord. Amen.

PRAYER OF GOOD WISH

O Lord Jesus, grant us goodness, the goodness of eye, the good-
ness of liking, the goodness of heart's desiring;

Grant us the goodness of sons, the goodness of daughters, the
goodness of pervading strength of mind;

Grant us the goodness of sea, the goodness of land, and thine own
goodness, thou Prince of heaven, who reignest for evermore.
Amen.

PRAYER AT UNDRESSING

O Great God, grant me thy light, thy grace, and thy happiness, and may I be made white in the well of thy health; lift, O God, from me my anguish, my loathing, and my vanity of vanities, lightening my soul in the light of thy love; as I take off my clothes, grant I take off my stresses; as the mists lift from the mountain-tops, so do thou lift my soul from the breath of dying;

And, O Jesus Christ Son of Mary, O Jesus Christ Paschal Son, shield my body in the shielding of thy clothing, and make white my soul in the whitening of thy grace;

I ask this for Jesus Christ his sake. Amen.

SHIELDING PRAYER

O God, we pray thee hearken unto our prayer and let our cry come unto thee, for we know that thou dost hear us as though we saw thee with our eyes;

We are setting a look upon our heart, upon our thoughts, upon our lips, and double we bind them;

Aught that is wrong for our soul when our death is throbbing, do thou, O God, sweep it from us, our shield in the blood of thy love, nor let thought to our heart, sound to our ear, temptation to our eye, fragrance to our nostril, fancy to our mind, or ripple to our spirit come to hurt our poor bodies this night, come to injure our souls at death's hour;

But be thou thyself, O God of life, at our breast and behind us, a star and guiding from the beginning of life to its ending, through Jesus Christ our Lord. Amen.

REST BLESSING

O God, bless our dwelling and each one who rests here tonight; bless, O God, our dear ones in each place that they sleep; in the evening that makes tonight and in every single evening, and in the day that is today and in every single day, through Jesus Christ our Lord. Amen.

FROM HOME

On mountainside,
By falling burn,
God to provide,
At every turn,

On the cliff-edge
God be the rope,
God be the ledge,
God be the hope.

Upon the wave,
And in the storm,
God's hand to save,
God's love to warm.

When far away
God keep from fear,
God every day,
God present near.

PRAYER FOR A JOURNEY

O God, bless us this very day, this very night; bless to us, O thou God of grace, each day and season that is ours; bless the path on which we go, the earth that meets our step, and bless, O God, and give thy love to us; O God of gods, bless our rest and quiet, through Jesus Christ our Lord. Amen.

THE TRUE WAY

Be my path this day with God, my path with Christ, my path
with the Spirit, the Threefold Trinity all-kindly, ho, ho, ho!
all-kindly;

Be I shielded this day from evil, this night from harm, in both
my soul and my body, ho, ho, ho! by the Father, by the Son,
by the Holy Ghost;

The Father my shield, the Son my shield, the Spirit my shield, as
Three and as One, ho, ho, ho! as Three and as One,

God reigning for evermore. Amen.

BLESSING FOR A JOURNEY

O God, bless to us the earth that meets our step, the path on which
we go, the prayer of our desire, blessing also, O thou Timeless
One as a moon of moons, our rest;

And bless the thing of our hope, the thing of our love, the thing
of our faith, blessing, O King of kings, to us our eyes and look-
ing, through Jesus Christ our Lord. Amen.

DEPARTURE BLESSING

May the joy of God be in our face, a joy to all who see it, the encompassing of God around our neck, the angels of God our shielding; may the joy of night and day be ours, of sun and moon, of men and women, each land and sea of our travels; may every clime give happiness, give light and give gladness, the Son of the Virgin Mary at peace with us;

And may the encompassing of the God of life, of the Christ of love, of the Spirit Holy, befriend and help us, for ever and ever. Amen.

RANGING BLESSING

May the King shield us in the glen, may Christ keep us on the mountain, may the Spirit bathe us on the slope, as hollow, hill and plain we cross, as mountain, glen and strath we cross, in the name of the Three who live and reign, One God, for ever. Amen.

OCEAN BLESSING

O God, Father almighty of kindness, Jesus the Son of tears and of sorrow, and O Holy Spirit, with thine aid aiding, the ever living, ever great and everlasting Trinity, who brought the children of Israel through the Red Sea, and Jonah to land from the belly of the great monster of the ocean, who brought Saint Paul and his company in the ship from the torment of the sea and the beating of the waves, from the greatness of the storm and the heaviness of the weather, and when the tempest poured down on the Sea of Galilee, the waters were stilled;

Save us, free us and sanctify us; be thou, O King of the elements, seated at our helm, and lead us in peace to our journey's quest, with winds that are mild and kind, smiling and fragrant, no current, no whirlpool, no eddy to work harm upon us,

We ask all things of thee, O God, according to thine own will and word, through Jesus Christ our Lord. Amen.

NIGHT-SHIELDING PRAYER

Almighty Lord and God of power, shield and sustain us this night, this night, O God, and every evening, saving and loosing us from mischief and sinning, saving us, soul and body, each darkness and light;

Bless the land we hope to reach, the thing our eye of faith doth see, O God of life, blessing our state;

And bless the journey we make, the earth we tread, the matter of our going, O King of glory, blessing our state, through Jesus Christ our Lord. Amen.

BLESSING OF THE WATCHING SHEPHERD

O great God, with thine eye, with the eye of the God of Glory, the eye of the Virgin's Son, the eye of the gentle Spirit, aid us and shepherd us at all times, and pour down blessings upon us gently and generously, through the same Son of the Virgin, Jesus Christ our Lord. Amen.

SAFE-KEEPING

O Father, be near,
Thy guiding to steer,
Thy compassing here,
Thy love to endear,
When dangers appear.

O Christ, whom we see
Outstretched on the tree,
O save and set free
From sins wounding thee,
Compassionate be.

O Spirit so wise,
Thy blessing arise
That safety supplies,
A shield to our eyes
When horrors surprise.

God, we are thy sheep,
Thy rod the safe-keep,
If up the heart leap,
If sorrowed we weep,
Awake or asleep.

GOD'S ENCOMPASSING

O God, be thy sanctuary and thy right hand around us, on our flesh and on our frame, the sanctuary of the Holy King and the grace of the Holy Trinity upon us abiding always for evermore;

And be the sanctuary of the Holy Three shielding our whole life, this day and this night, from hate and harm, from good and evil, henceforth and for ever. Amen.

BLESSING FROM HEAVEN

O God, may the most dear love of the angels and of the saints, the most dear love of heaven, be our guarding our cherishing, through Jesus Christ our Lord. Amen.

UPLAND BLESSING

May God shield us by each sheer drop, may Christ keep us on each rock-path, may the Spirit fill us on each bare slope, as we cross hill and plain, who live and reign One God for ever. Amen.

BLESSING FROM ABOVE

O God, grant unto us the dear love of heaven and of the saints
and of the angels, the dear love of the sun and of the moon,
each day and night of our lives,

That we may be kept from them that hate, from them that
injure, and from them that oppress, through Jesus Christ our
Lord. Amen.

HEAVENLY BLESSING

O God of all life and of goodness, may the great company of the saints, the men and the women in the heavenly places, be with us in spirit in every strait, in every direction, and in every turn of our pilgrimage, through Jesus Christ our Lord. Amen.

SHRINE OF THE SOUL

O God, give commandment to thy blessed angels to make compassing of this steading tonight, a company devoted, mighty, and steadfast to keep this shrine of the soul from harm;

Safeguard, O God, this household tonight, its persons, its means of life, its good name, delivering it from death, from danger, from harm, and from the harvest of envy and hatred;

And, O God of peace, do thou grant us thankfulness with any loss, that we obey thy laws below and enjoy thyself in the beyond, where thou reignest for ever and ever. Amen.

HOURS OF DARKNESS

Watch over us, O thou God of the moon,
*   Shed down upon us thy lovely light,*
The darkness of evening is here too soon
*   If with thy presence it be not bright.*

Watch over us, O thou Son of the stars,
*   Whose foot once descended to the earth,*
And the darkness lightened as the great bars
*   Were withdrawn to admit of thy birth.*

Watch over us, O thou Spirit of light,
*   Let shine effulgent grace for the eye,*
Protect us throughout the darkness of night
*   Underneath the black roof of the sky.*

Watch over us now, O Holy Three,
*   Tonight we lay us down to our rest,*
Lying down our host-companions may it be
*   That with God's peacefulness we be blest.*

THE GIFTS OF THE HOLY TRINITY

O Holy blessed Trinity, may the Spirit give us of his abundance, the Father of his wisdom, the Son Jesus in our need give the shelter of his shield;

For we lie down tonight with the Trinity of power, with the Father, with Jesus, with the Spirit of virtues, who live and reign One God, world without end. Amen.

NEW MOON PETITION

O King of the elements, bless, we beseech thee, the new moon appearing, that fragrant be every night on which she shines, that her light be full to all in need, her path obscured not to all beset, her light above to all in distress, her guiding below to all in need;

And grant that the moon of moons come through the thick clouds, come to us and to all through the tears of darkness, God's hand dwelling with us in every strait that befalls us, now and till the hour of our death, and till the day of our resurrection, through Jesus Christ our Lord. Amen.

BLESSING AT RETIRING

O God, bless to us the moon above our heads, the ground beneath our feet; bless our partner and our children, and ourselves who have the care of them;

O God, bless that which comes to our eyes, that which comes to our hope, and bless our thinking and our desire, O God of all life;

O God, bless those who sleep beneath our roof, bless the things our hands do, bless the sanctity of our sanctuary, and bless the angel of our sleep, O God, through Jesus Christ our Lord. Amen.

PRAYER OF SLEEP

Soul and body, O God, we set ourselves in the protection of thy holy place, of thy holy place, O Jesus Christ, of thy holy place, O Spirit of clear truth, the Three who stand in our defence nor turn their backs upon us;

O Father, thou who art kind and just, O Son, thou who didst overcome sin, thou, O Holy Spirit of might, keep us this night from mischief, thou Three who uphold justice for us, keeping us this night and always,

O blessed Trinity, who reignest world without end. Amen.

PUTTING OUT THE LIGHT

O God of life, darken not thy light to us, nor close the joy, nor shut to us thy door;

O God of life, withhold not thy forgiveness, quench thy disdain of us,

And, O God of life, crown to us thy rejoicing comfort, thy rejoicing comfort, O God of life, through Jesus Christ our Lord. Amen.

THE WORLD OF REPOSE

O thou Being of virtues wonderful, shield us with thy might, O thou Law-giver Being and of the stars; encompass us tonight soul and body, encompass us tonight and every night;

Encompass us justly between earth and heaven, between the mystery of thy laws and our eyes of blindness, between what we see and what we take not in, between what is clear and what is not clear in our heart's desire; we ask this through Jesus Christ our Lord. Amen.

PEACE-BLESSING FOR LIFE

The peace of God and of Jesus and of the Spirit be upon us and upon our children, O upon us and upon our children, each day and night of our portion in the world. Amen.

THE WORLD YONDER

As a swan, wounded, waiting,
As a drake of migrating,
As a dove, indicating
The Holy Ghostly sating,
So the soul will wing away
From this marsh of earthly day;

As a waif, lost and straying,
Orphan-child of dismaying,
As a bondman obeying,
As a wretch dumbly praying,
So the soul lies at the gate
Over the river of its fate;

As a spark, fitful flaring,
As a gust, falter-faring,
As a wraith, startled staring,
As a trail-smoke, smudge-bearing,
So the soul slips from its frame
Guttered as a candle-flame;

With a word, gentle greeting,
With a wing, Michael meeting,
With a hand at entreating,
With an arm, Christ completing,
Brought before the bar of light,
Grant it may be clothed in white.

DEATH PRAYER

O God, grant unto us of thy wisdom, of thy compassion, of thy
plentifulness, and of thy guidance in face of every difficulty;

And, O God, grant unto us of thy holiness, of thine assistance, of
thine encircling, and of thy repose in the tangle of our death,
of thine encircling and of thy repose in the house of our death;
we ask this through Jesus Christ our Lord. Amen.

SUPPLICATION FOR THE SOUL

O Holy God of eternity, when our soul parts from the body of
wiles* and goes up in flashes of light from the body of this life,
come thou to seek us and to find us;

May God and Jesus help us, may God and Jesus defend us, may
God and Jesus seek us and find us for ever. Amen.

**Wiles.* Cunning contrivance and artifice.

PRAYER AT THE NEW MOON

O Being of the elements, when we see the new moon it is fitting
we say our prayer and give praise to thee for thy kindness and
goodness;

For many is the man and many is the woman who has gone
hence over the dark river of the abyss, since last the counten-
ance of the new moon of the heavens shone upon us; where-
fore we praise thee, through Jesus Christ our Lord. Amen.

DEATH-BED PRAYER

O Great God of salvation, pour down thy graces on our souls as the sun of the heights pours down its love on our bodies; for we must die though we know not the place nor the hour, and if we die without thy graces we are not lost for ever;

Grant us therefore a death of unction and of repentance, of rejoicing and of peace, of grace and of forgiveness, a death which gives heaven and life with Christ, in whose name we ask this. Amen.

JOURNEY PETITION

O God of life, do thou ease our way before us, a guide-star above
   us, a sharp eye behind us, this day, this night and for ever;
Through weariness and heaviness of spirit lead us to the land of
   the angels, for it is time we went for a season to the court of
   Christ, to the peace of heaven;
If only thou, O God, be at ease with us, be at our back, be as star,
   be as rudder, from our lying-down at ease to our rising anew,
   through the same Jesus Christ our Lord. Amen.

THANKSGIVING

Each step of joy we take
A song of praise we make,
A prayer of thanks is said
     From heart and head.

The sun and moon arise,
The wonders of the skies,
The stars and clouds are there
     For speaking fair.

We rise up safe at morn
To greet the light of dawn,
We lie down safe at night
     And laud aright.

We eat our daily bread,
We thank that we are fed,
We praise the majesty
     Of land and sea.

We sing the glory-birth
When Jesus came to earth,
We sing the glory-death
     With loving breath.

Praise to the Father be,
Praise to the Son, death-free,
Praise to the Holy Ghost,
     The Three foremost.

ETERNAL LIGHT

O God, who hast brought us from last night's resting to this morning's daylight of joy, do thou bring us from this morning's new daylight to the everlasting light that guideth, from the new morning daylight to the guiding light of the everlasting, through Jesus Christ our Lord. Amen.

MORNING PRAISE-PRAYER

O gentle Lord Christ, thanks be unto thee for ever in that thou hast raised us in freedom from the darkness and the terrors of the night unto the gentle light of this day;

O God of all living things, praise be unto thee for each gift of life that thou hast poured upon us, for our desires, our words, our senses, our praise with men, for our thoughts, our doings, our goings, and our fame, through the same Jesus Christ our Lord. Amen.

MORNING DEDICATION

O God, thanks be unto thee for bringing us from the day that is gone unto the beginning of this day with good intended that everlasting joy be purchased for our being;

For every gift of peace bestowed on us, for thoughts and speech, for deeds and for desires, we dedicate ourselves to thee;

And we make our supplication and our prayer that we be kept from sin and receive thine aid through the night that is to come, for the sake of the wounds of the sacrifice of grace of Jesus Christ thy Son our Lord. Amen.

PRAYER AT RISING

Bless, O God, to us the seeing of our eyes, the hearing of our ears, the smelling of our nostrils, and the tasting of our lips;

Bless the notes of our singing, the light of our going, the object of our pursuing, and the drawing of our following;

And may the zeal that seeks our living soul and the Holy Three that seek our heart be with our heart and living soul for evermore. Amen.

THE LIGHT OF THE DAY

O God, grant that the eye of thy greatness, the eye of thy glory,
the eye of the King of hosts, of the King of living things, shed
light upon us at each time and moment, shed light upon us
gently and fully;

All glory be to the blazing sun, to the sun of the face of the God
of the elements, who reigneth for ever. Amen.

THE GOD OF THUNDER

O God of the elements, of the mysteries, of the stars and cloud-
springs, King of kings, thy joy is the joy, thy light the light, thy
warring the war, and thy peace the peace; thy pain is the pain,
thy love the love that ever lasts to the end of endings; and thou
pourest thy grace on folk in bondage, on folk in straits, unceas-
ing and with full flow;

All glory to thee and to Jesus the Son of Mary, the Paschal One,
the Son of death, the Son of grace, who wast and shalt be with
the ebb and with the flow, with ebb and flow for ever. Amen.

THE LANTERN OF THE POOR

O God, in the name of the Father, and of the Son, and of the Spirit, the Holy Three of pity, for the bright moon of this night, that shineth for ever the glorious lantern of the poor, glory be unto thee, O God, for ever. Amen.

NATIVITY PRAISE

O God of the moon and of the sun, of the world and of the stars,
God of the waters, the land and the skies, who ordained for us
the King of promise, praise be unto thee;

For it was Saint Mary mild who brought forth the Being of Life
and set him in her bosom, darkness and tears set behind, the
star of guiding early on high;

The land shone forth, the earth shone forth, the doldrums and
current shone forth, grief was laid by and joy was raised while
music of harp and pedal played; all praise be unto thee for ever.
Amen.

THE CHRISTMAS NIGHT

O Great God of the night and of the day, praise be unto thee:

Praise be unto thee for this the long night of flake and drift, of white snow until the day, of a white moon until the dawn;

For this night the eve of the great birth when the Son was born to the Mary Virgin, Jesus thy son, O King of glory, who is the stock of our joy;

For this night when the sun edged the high hills with light, when sea and land were edged with light, when Christ the King of greatness was born;

Before the sound of the glory coming was known, the sound of the wave was on the strand, before the sound of his footfall upon the ground was known, the sound of the song of the glorious angels rang forth on this long night;

Wood and tree were shining, hill and water, field and vale were shining when his step came to the earth; all praise be unto thee. Amen.

THE LIGHT OF THE NIGHT

O God of the elements, glory be unto thee because of the moon guide-lantern of the ocean:

Grant us thine own hand on our rudder-helm and thy love behind on the great heaving waters, through Jesus Christ our Lord. Amen.